Lerner SPORTS

SPORTS
ALL-STARS

ODELL BECKHAM JR.

Anthony K. Hewson

Lerner Publications ◆ Minneapolis

Lerner Publications Company
A division of Lerner Publishing Group, Inc.
241 First Avenue North
Minneapolis, MN 55401 USA

For reading levels and more information, look up this title at www.lernerbooks.com.

Main body text set in Albany Std.
Typeface provided by Agfa.

Library of Congress Cataloging-in-Publication Data
Names: Hewson, Anthony K., author.
Title: Odell Beckham Jr. / by Anthony K. Hewson.
Description: Minneapolis : Lerner Publications, [2020] | Series: Sports All-Stars |
    Audience: Ages: 7–11. | Audience: Grades: K to Grade 3. | Includes webography. |
    Includes bibliographical references and index.
Identifiers: LCCN 2018059340 (print) | LCCN 2019000455 (ebook) |
    ISBN 9781541556256 (eb pdf) | ISBN 9781541556157 (library binding : alk.
    paper) | ISBN 9781541574519 (paperback : alk. paper)
Subjects: LCSH: Beckham, Odell, Jr., 1992—-Juvenile literature. | Football players—
    United States—Biography—Juvenile literature.
Classification: LCC GV939.B424 (ebook) | LCC GV939.B424 H49 2019 (print) | DDC
    796.332092 [B] —dc23

LC record available at https://lccn.loc.gov/2018059340

Manufactured in the United States of America
1-CG-7/15/19

CONTENTS

CATCH
OF THE YEAR

Beckham (right) poses for a photo after being drafted by the Giants.

New York Giants fans could not wait to watch Odell Beckham Jr. He was the Giants' top pick in the 2014 National Football League (NFL) Draft. Fans wanted to see what he could do. But Beckham was injured at the start of the 2014 season. He missed the first four games.

- **Date of Birth:** November 5, 1992

- **Position:** wide receiver

- **League:** NFL

- **Professional Highlights:** drafted 12th overall by the New York Giants in 2014; won NFL Offensive **Rookie** of the Year; made the Pro Bowl in each of his first three seasons; traded to the Cleveland Browns in 2019

- **Personal Highlights:** attended the same college as his parents; enjoys fashion; had a small acting role in the TV show *Code Black*; has been in music videos with Drake, Nicki Minaj, and Ariana Grande

Beckham became famous for his catch on November 23, 2014.

He turned out to be worth the wait. The way Beckham caught the football dazzled fans. It seemed like no catch was too difficult for him. His greatest catch of the season came on November 23, when the Giants played the Dallas Cowboys. The two teams were big **rivals**. More than 20 million people watched the game on TV. Beckham caught a touchdown on the Giants' first **drive** of the game.

On the first play of the second quarter, Giants quarterback Eli Manning looked Beckham's way again. He threw a pass deep toward the end zone. Beckham jumped for the ball. The Cowboys' **defense** tried to hold him back.

As the ball headed out of bounds, Beckham reached as far back as he could with one hand. He grabbed the ball with just a few fingers of his right hand and pulled it to his chest. Then he fell to the ground. Touchdown!

The catch thrilled fans. Former NFL receiver Cris Collinsworth talked about the game on TV. He said it was the greatest catch he had ever seen. Famous athletes such as basketball player LeBron James reacted with amazement on social media. The catch turned Beckham into a superstar.

"I didn't notice right at the moment," Beckham said, "but after everything settled down it kind of all hit me. . . . Things haven't been the same since then."

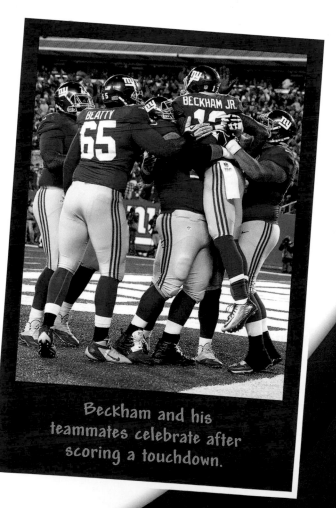

Beckham and his teammates celebrate after scoring a touchdown.

THREE-SPORT STAR

Odell was a star on his high school football team.

A lot of kids who grow up in Louisiana become fans of the Louisiana State University (LSU) Tigers. Odell Beckham Jr. was no different. But his ties to LSU were stronger than most.

Odell was born November 5, 1992, in Baton Rouge, Louisiana, where LSU is located. His parents were both students at the time, and they both played sports for the Tigers. His dad played football, and his mom ran track.

Odell was athletic like his parents. He wanted to

Odell (right) and his father, Odell Beckham Sr., attend an event together in 2018.

succeed like them. Growing up, Odell played football and ran track like his parents. He also played basketball. He was great at all three.

At Isidore Newman High School in New Orleans, Odell earned **letters** in all three sports. But football was where he shined the most. He caught 50 passes for 1,110 yards and 19 touchdowns as a senior.

He was only the second player in school history to break 1,000 receiving yards.

Odell could play any position on the field. He played running back, quarterback, receiver, punt returner, kick returner, and cornerback. Many college teams wanted Odell because he was so talented. But he chose to attend LSU.

Playing football in college was more difficult for Odell than it had been in high school. He was not the best player right away. But he worked hard as a receiver and punt returner. He was second on the team in receiving yards as a freshman. He was a team leader the following year and one of the nation's top receivers by the next.

Star NFL quarterbacks and brothers Peyton and Eli Manning also went to Isidore Newman High School. Eli and Odell ended up as teammates on the Giants.

Odell skipped his senior season at LSU and entered the 2014 NFL Draft. The New York Giants chose him. He was the 12th player chosen overall.

The teams that passed on Odell soon regretted it. He had one of the best rookie seasons in NFL history. He played in only 12 games but still caught 91 passes for 1,305 yards and 12 touchdowns. No other NFL player had ever had more catches and yards in his first 12 games.

Odell was an LSU Tiger like his parents.

Odell's catches quickly made him an NFL star.

Odell tries to break a tackle during a game against the Philadelphia Eagles.

But those numbers only told part of the story. With his amazing one-handed catch in November, Odell gave fans something they had never seen before. He was a player who could always do something incredible.

Beckham warms up before a game in 2018.

Beckham has two things that any receiver would love to have. He has speed, and he has big hands. Beckham is not the largest or the tallest receiver in the NFL. He's 5 feet 11 inches (1.8 m) tall and weighs 198 pounds (90 kg).

Beckham practices catches before a game.

But he can jump. Even if a taller player is guarding him, he can usually jump higher and snatch the ball.

Beckham's big hands are perfect for catching a football. But how big are they exactly? In 2015 some sportswriters decided to find out. They gave Beckham a few different types of objects to hold. He could hold 10 golf balls in a single hand. With both hands, he could hold 376 almonds.

Beckham doesn't just rely on his natural talent to play great football. He works hard in practice and in the gym to get stronger. Before every game and in every practice, he works on catching the football.

Even when he played with LSU, Beckham was known for working hard during practice and warmups.

When he was at LSU, Beckham and teammate Jarvis Landry used to sneak into the indoor practice field after hours. They wanted to practice with a machine that would pass the ball to them. They used the machine so much that it broke.

"On Friday nights, when everybody else was going and hanging out, they were there catching footballs," LSU receivers coach Adam Henry said.

As a receiver, Beckham needs to move fast. To work on this, he does an exercise called the speed ladder. A fabric ladder is placed on the ground. Beckham runs through it as fast as he can, stepping each foot in each rung of the ladder once before moving forward.

Hand-eye coordination is also very important for a receiver. Beckham works on this with a unique drill.

He stands in front of his **trainer**. The trainer tosses tennis balls to the left and right of Beckham. The trainer changes the side he tosses them from and how he delivers them. Beckham has to react quickly and change directions to keep catching the tennis balls.

Beckham is a **gifted** athlete. But his hard work and practice keep him at the top of the NFL.

Beckham throws the ball while warming up before a 2018 game.

Beckham is famous for his one-handed catches. He set a world record in 2015. He caught 33 passes with one hand in a single minute.

Off the field,
Beckham is
known for his fun
fashion choices.

Beckham often wears shoes with different colors or patterns while playing.

Beckham stands out on the field because of his catches. But people notice him off the field as well.

Beckham loves fashion. His interest started in middle school. All of Beckham's friends were wearing suits to a dance, but he wanted to stand out.

Beckham talks onstage at the Nickelodeon Kids' Choice Sports Awards in 2017.

So he wore a pink velvet jacket instead. Beckham still makes **bold** fashion choices. It's his way of sharing who he is.

"I'm weird," Beckham said. "I think I just naturally stand out."

Another part of Beckham's style is his tattoos. He is almost totally covered in them from head to toe. Some are personal. Some show people he admires, such as boxing legend Muhammad Ali and President Barack Obama.

Beckham also shows who he is through **charity** work. He has worked with the Make-a-Wish Foundation to help sick children. He has also worn special shoes with the Make-a-Wish logo on them to promote the organization.

Beckham was 12 years old when Hurricane Katrina destroyed his hometown of New Orleans. In 2017 he gave $100,000 to help victims of Hurricane Harvey after it struck Houston, Texas. He also encouraged all Americans to give what they could to help.

Beckham greets a young fan before a game against the Dallas Cowboys.

Beckham (right) and rapper A$AP Rocky hang out at a fashion show in New York City.

Beckham also loves music and is friends with the rapper Drake. Beckham has showed off his dance moves in one of Drake's music videos. He has also been in a video with Nicki Minaj and Ariana Grande. Beckham loves life and enjoys showing how much fun he is having.

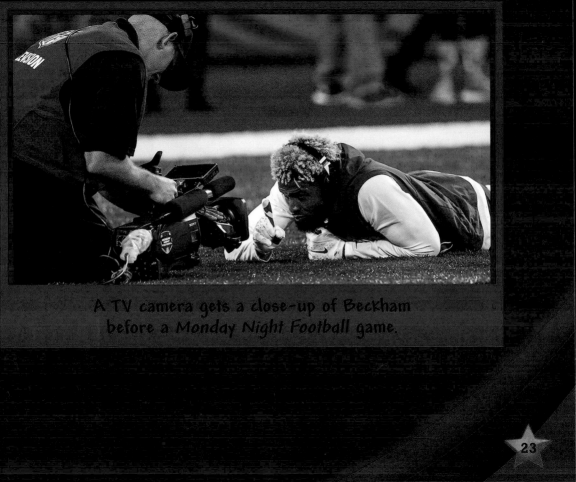

A TV camera gets a close-up of Beckham before a *Monday Night Football* game.

NFL RECORD BREAKER

Beckham played for the New York Giants for the first five seasons of his NFL career.

Few teams have been around as long as the Giants. They have had many great players. But in just a few short years, Beckham became one of their best ever. At the end of the 2018 season, Beckham ranked second in receiving yards, fourth in catches, and fourth in receiving touchdowns in team history.

From 2014 to 2016, Beckham led the NFL in touchdown receptions. He was the first player in NFL history to have 80 catches and 1,000 receiving yards in each of his first three seasons. Beckham was NFL Offensive Rookie of the Year in 2014 and played in three straight Pro Bowls.

Beckham accepts the 2014 NFL Offensive Rookie of the Year Award.

He was a record-setting machine.

The only thing that slowed him down was an injury. In 2017 Beckham was on his way to another 1,000-yard season. In a game against the Los Angeles Chargers, he jumped to catch a high pass. But as he landed, his left foot twisted underneath him. Beckham broke his ankle.

Medics help Beckham off the field after he was injured in a 2017 game.

He had to miss the rest of the season. This was hard for him, but he stayed strong. He wrote a message to fans on social media. "Thank u all for your prayers," he wrote. "You better believe I'll be back better than ever. God Speed."

Beckham was ready to play by the start of the 2018 season. He was running and jumping with no problems. In his first game back, he caught 11 passes for 111 yards.

There was just one thing missing from Beckham's achievements. During his first five seasons, he had played in only one **playoff** game. The Giants lost 38–13 to the Green Bay Packers to end their 2016 season. Beckham caught just four passes for 28 yards during that game.

After the 2018 season, New York decided it was time to rebuild its roster and traded Beckham to the Cleveland Browns. The Browns had a talented young team. Beckham was excited about the opportunity to help them reach their first Super Bowl.

Beckham reaches to catch the ball during a game against the San Francisco 49ers.

All-Star Stats

Beckham has had a great career so far. In his first 42 career games, he was one of only two players since 1950 to reach 4,000 receiving yards. Here is where he ranked after 42 games.

Most Receiving Yards After 42 Games

1. Lance Alworth, 4,094 yards
2. Odell Beckham Jr., 4,078 yards
3. Charley Hennigan, 3,949 yards
4. Harlon Hill, 3,653 yards
5. Randy Moss, 3,646 yards
6. Anquan Boldin, 3,526 yards
7. Julio Jones, 3,471 yards
8. Homer Jones, 3,440 yards
9. (tie) A.J. Green, 3,427 yards
9. (tie) Jerry Rice, 3,427 yards

Source Notes

7. Howie Kussoy, "The Oral History of the Catch that Made Odell Beckham Legend," *New York Post*, September 12, 2015, https://nypost.com/2015/09/12/the-oral-history-of-the-catch-that-made-odell-beckham-legend/

16. Ebenezer Samuel, "LSU Coaches Wanted Odell Beckham Jr. and Jarvis Landry to Stop Making One-Handed Catches," *New York Daily News*, December 14, 2015, http://www.nydailynews.com/sports/football/giants/lsu-coaches-begged-beckham-landry-catch-hands-article-1.2465525

20. Jamle Lisanti, "Odell Beckham Jr. Stands Out in Style," *Sports Illustrated*, July 10, 2018, https://www.si.com/lifestyle/2018/07/10/odell-beckham-jr-fashionable-50-2018-cover

26. Kevin Hickey, "Giants' Odell Beckham Jr.: 'I'll Be Back Better Than Ever,'" *USA Today*, October 10, 2017. https://giantswire.usatoday.com/2017/10/10/new-york-giants-odell-beckham-jr-ankle-surgery-season-ending-ill-be-back/

Glossary

bold: something unique, unusual, or daring

charity: related to an organization that helps other people or raises money for a good cause

debut: a first public appearance or performance

defense: in football, the team that doesn't have the ball and tries to prevent the other team from scoring

drive: a series of plays that move the football down the field toward the opponent's end zone

film producer: a person in charge of making a movie

gifted: having a special, natural ability to do something

letters: awards given to high school students for achievement in sports or other activities

playoff: a series of games after the regular season that determine which teams will compete for the championship

rivals: two or more people who are competing against one another

rookie: an athlete who is in his first season with a professional sports team

trainer: someone who helps people, especially athletes, exercise and get in shape

Further Information

Fishman, Jon M. *Odell Beckham Jr.* Minneapolis: Lerner
Publications, 2017.

Gitlin, Marty. *Odell Beckham Jr.: Football Star.* Mankato, MN:
North Star Editions, 2017.

Kelley, K. C. *Odell Beckham Jr.* New York: Bearport
Publishing Company, Inc., 2016.

Odell Beckham Jr. College Stats
https://www.sports-reference.com/cfb/players/odell-beckham-jr-1.html

Odell Beckham Jr. Cleveland Browns Bio
https://www.clevelandbrowns.com/team/players-roster/odell-beckham-jr

Odell Beckham Jr. Pro Stats
https://www.pro-football-reference.com/players/B/BeckOd00.htm

Index

Photo Acknowledgments

The images in this book are used with the permission of: © Rich Kane/Icon SMI/ Corbis/Icon Sportswire/Getty Images, pp. 4–5; © Al Bello/Getty Images Sport/Getty Images, pp. 6, 7, 19; © Seth Poppel/Yearbook Library, p. 8; © Jstone/Shutterstock. com, p. 9; © Sean Gardner/Getty Images Sport/Getty Images, p. 11; © Tom Pennington/Getty Images Sport/Getty Images, pp. 12, 17; © Focus on Sport/Getty Images Sport/Getty Images, p. 13; © Mike Lawrie/Getty Images Sport/Getty Images, p. 14; © Bob Levey/Getty Images Sport/Getty Images, p. 15; © Stacy Revere/Getty Images Sport/Getty Images, p 16; © David Crotty/Patrick McMullan/Getty Images, p. 18; © Kevin Winter/Getty Images Entertainment/Getty Images, p. 20; © Jim Cowsert/Fort Worth Star-Telegram/TNS/Tribune News Service/Getty Images, p. 21; © Nicholas Hunt/Getty Images Entertainment/Getty Images, p. 22; © Rich Graessle/ Icon Sportswire/Getty Images, p. 23; © Rich Graessle/Icon Sportswire/Corbis/Getty Images, p. 24; © Kevin Mazur/WireImage/Getty Images, p. 25; © Jeff Zelevansky/ Getty Images Sport/Getty Images, p. 26; © Thearon W. Henderson/Getty Images Sport/Getty Images, p. 27.

Front Cover: © Joe Robbins/Getty Images Sport/Getty Images.